Healing With Art....
Pain, Trauma, Healing

Author/Artist
Christina Scafidi Adams

Wisdom Wall

1. Be childlike not childish
2. Private life influences public life
3. Real faith is maturity
4. Respect proper boundaries
5. Transformation without application is impossible
6. Sowing discord is evil
7. Don't stir strife
8. Proverbs is insight into wisdom
9. Foolishness is wicked, righteousness is wise
10. Wisdom is a person named Jesus
11. Delayed obedience is disobedience
12. To quench is failing to do something correctly
13. Wisdom is invitation to bring in revelation
14. Church is the kingdom and our bodies are the church
15. Wisdom builds
16. Don't give time to mockers
17. Real spirituality is practical
18. Be easily corrected
19. Rain in life not over people
20. Sow righteousness not wickedness
21. Wisdom apart from action is not wisdom
22. Knowledge is potential power

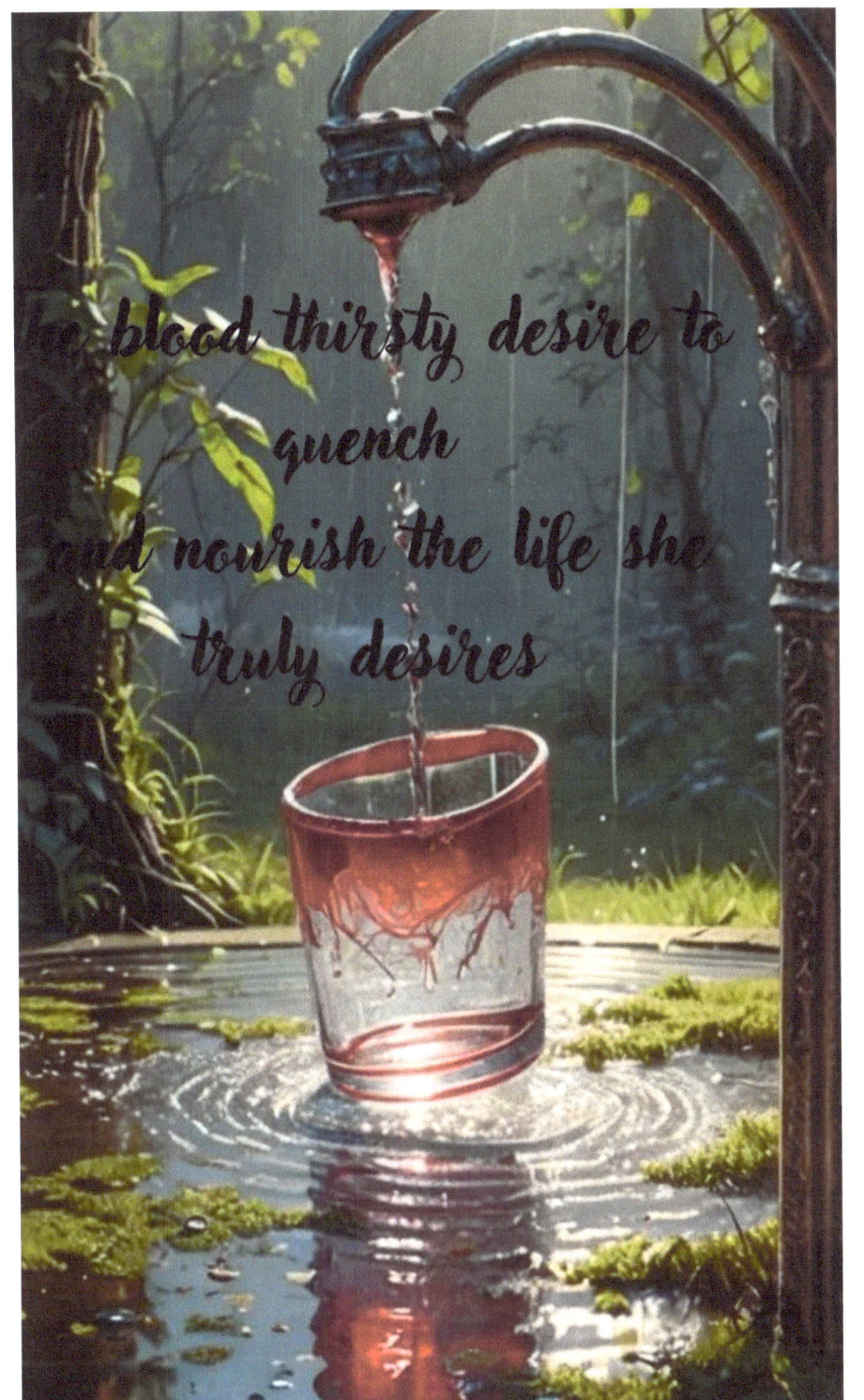

The beautiful rose, some look at her thorns and see a dangerous weapon, when in reality those thorns are guarding her from the enemies that might pick her and cause her demise.

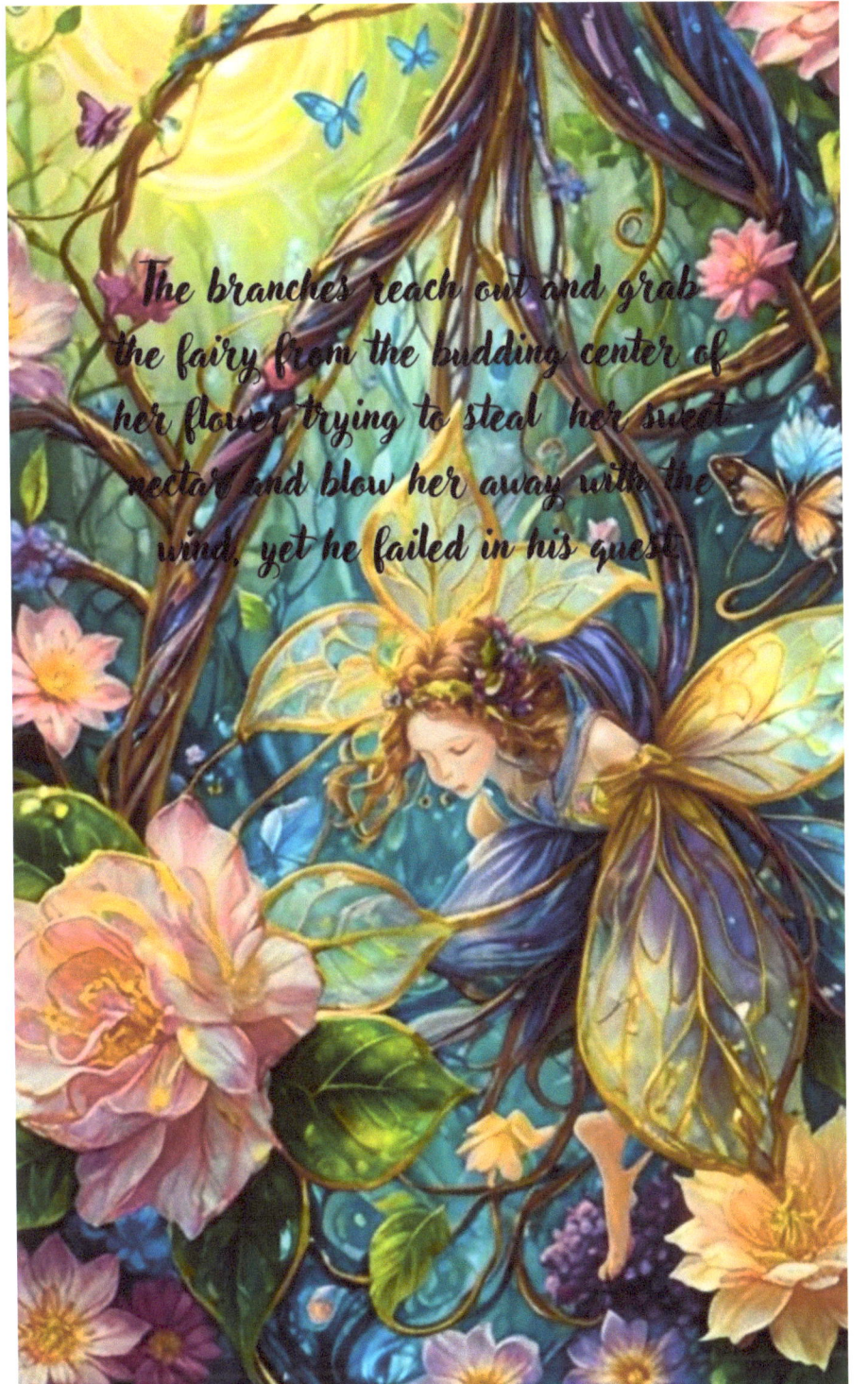

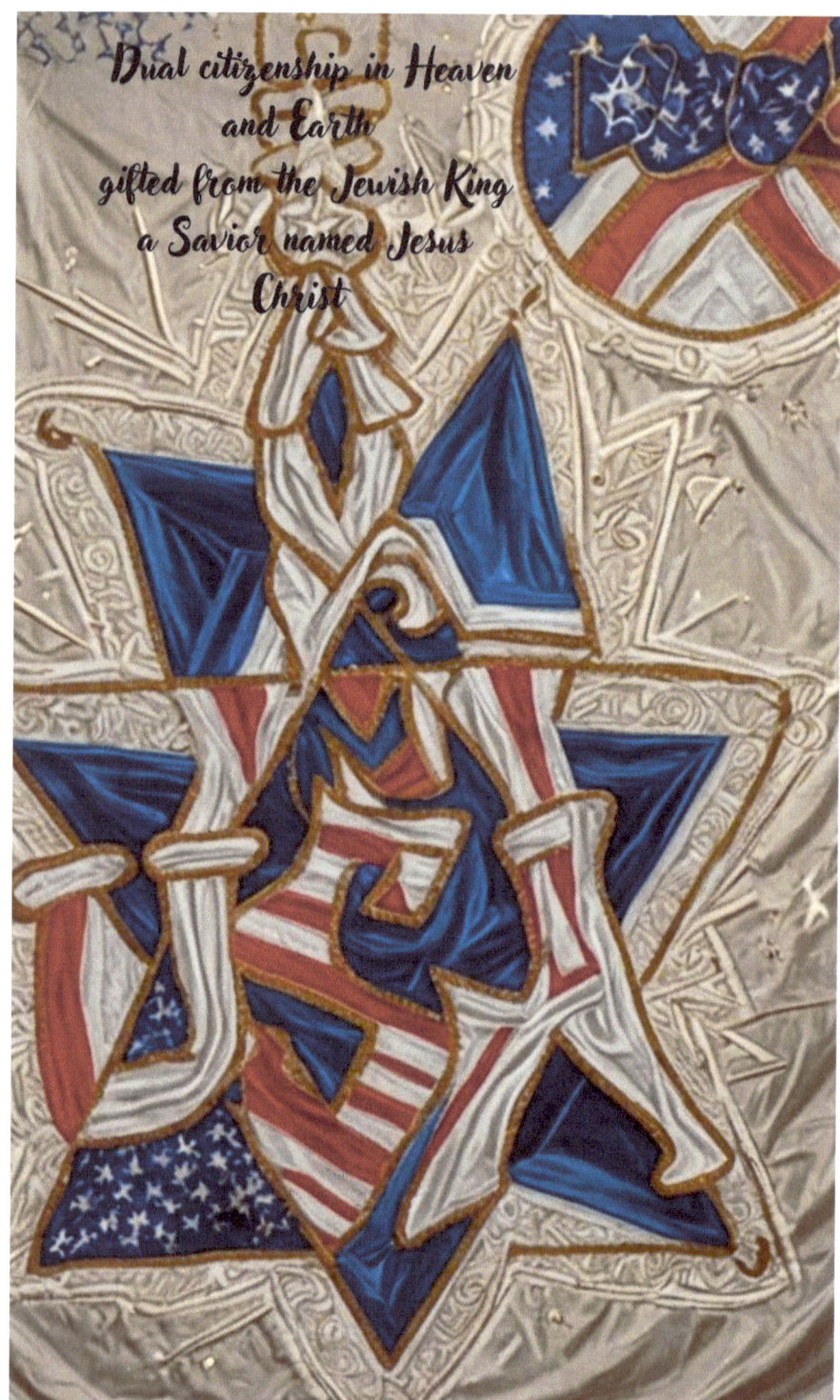

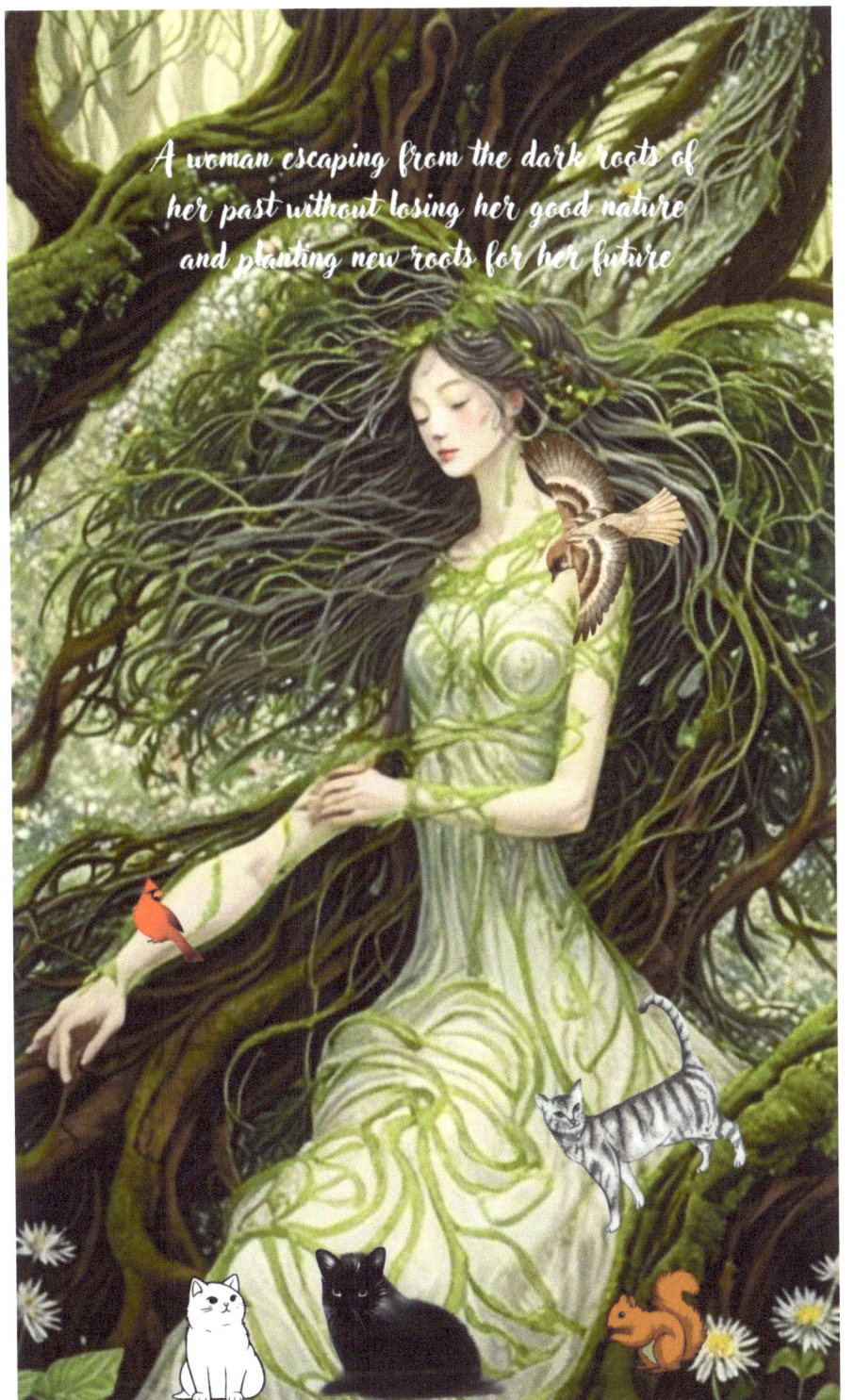

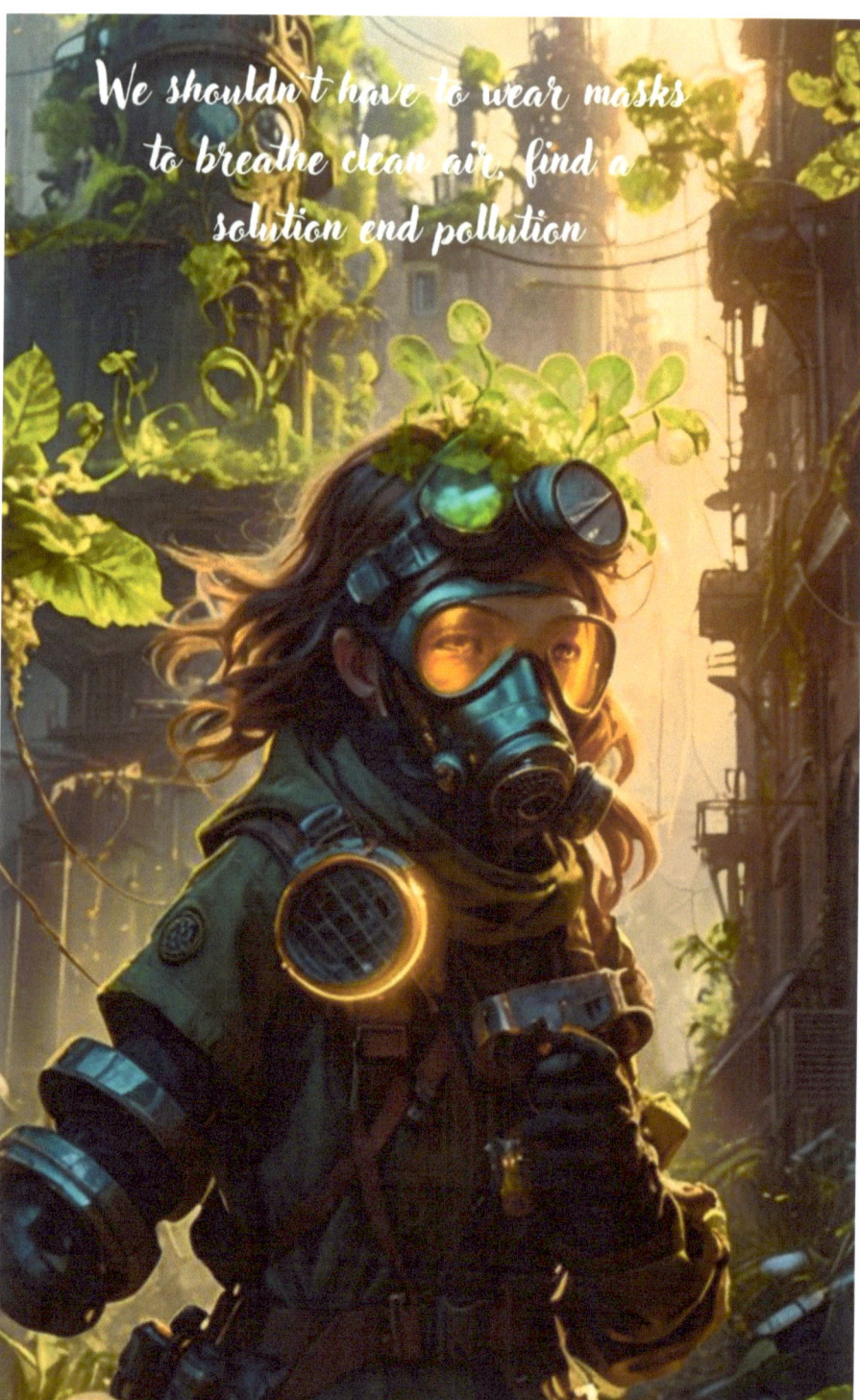

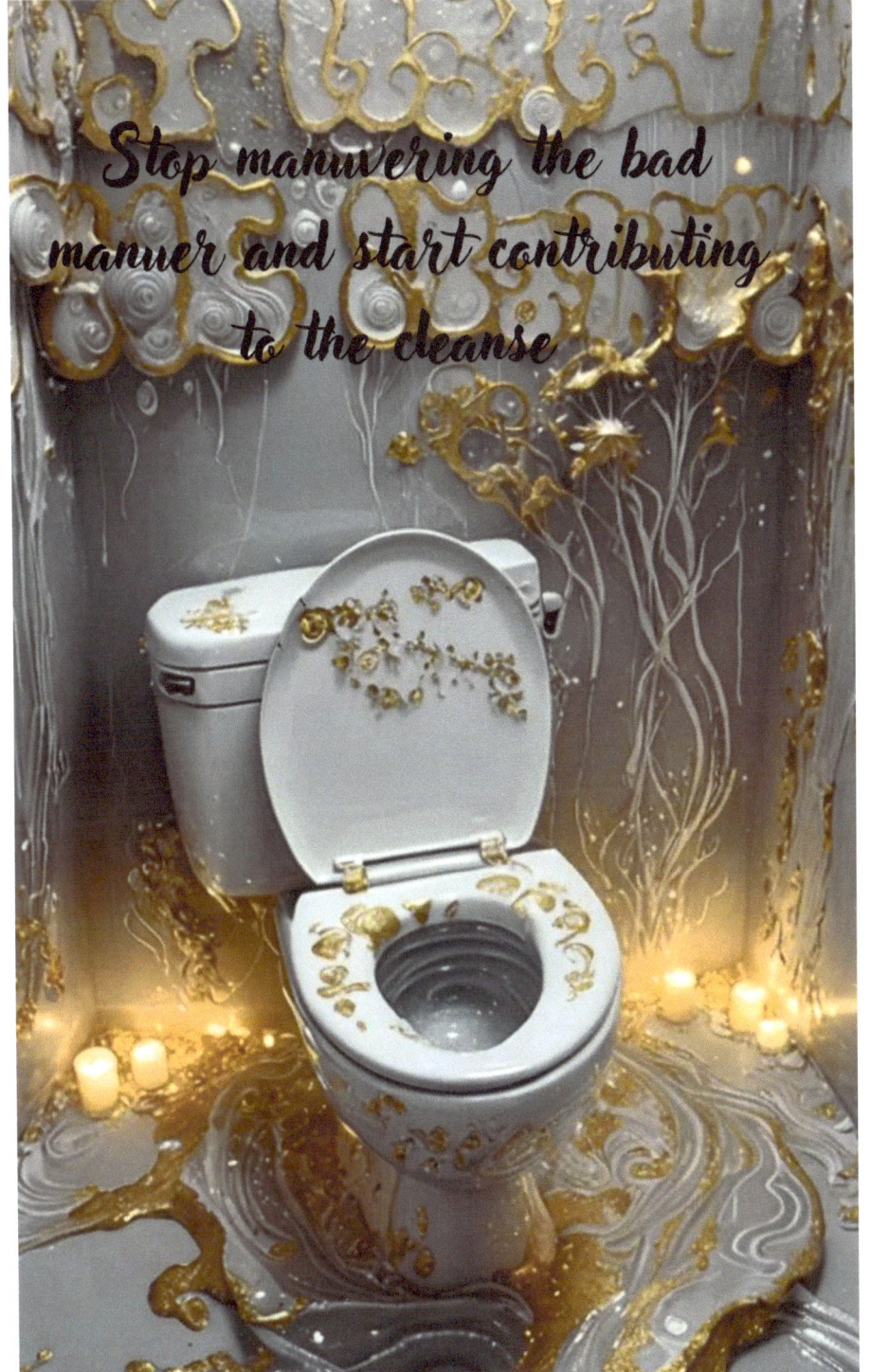

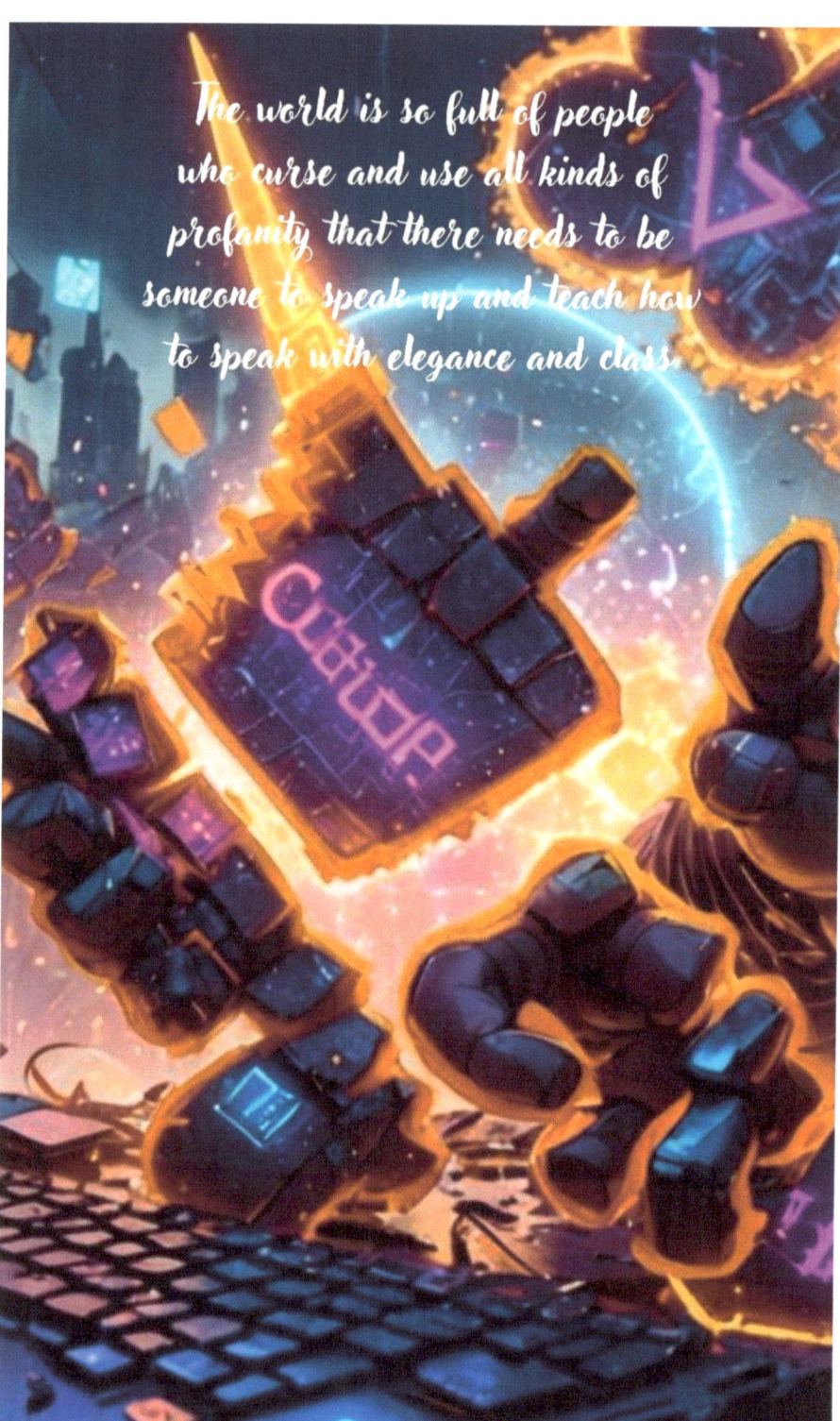

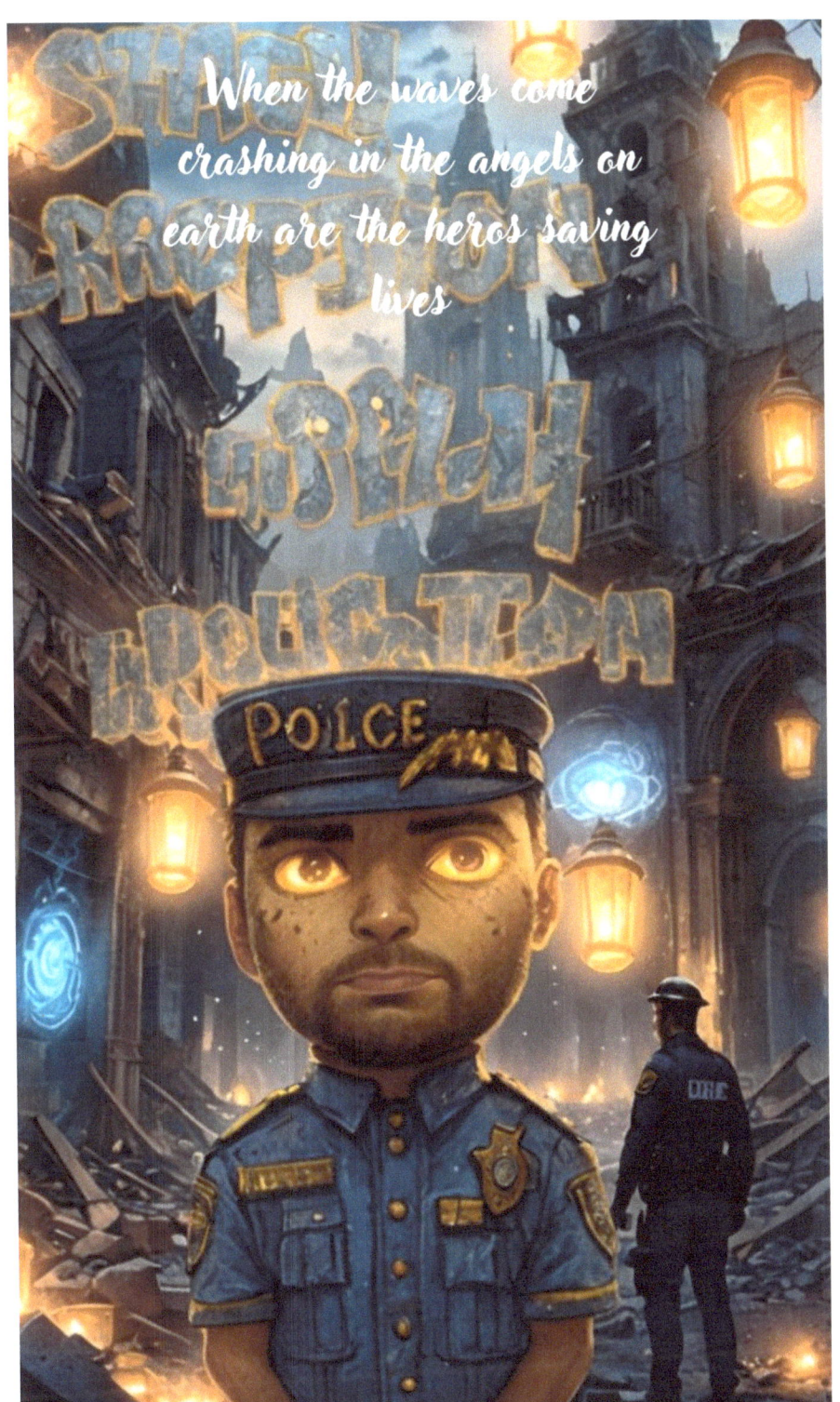

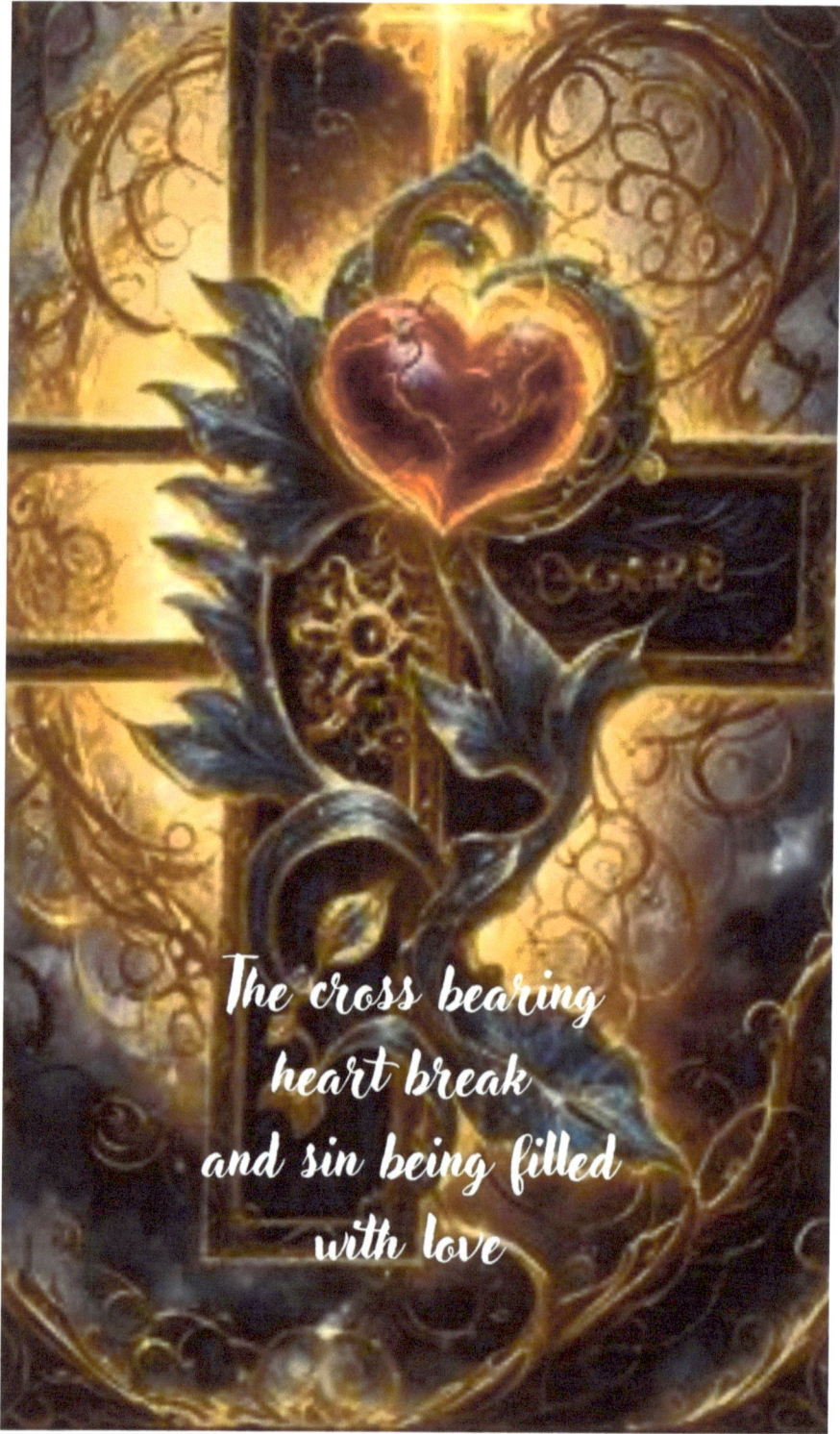

The musical stiletto with violin shaped legs creating music with every step she takes, the click of her heels sets off a beat and rhythm in someones musical composition creating an orchestra of beautiful sheet music in the hearts of strangers

The flower in the garden hidden behind the sadness in her eyes to afraid to blossom and show the world her beauty fearing they might break her heart

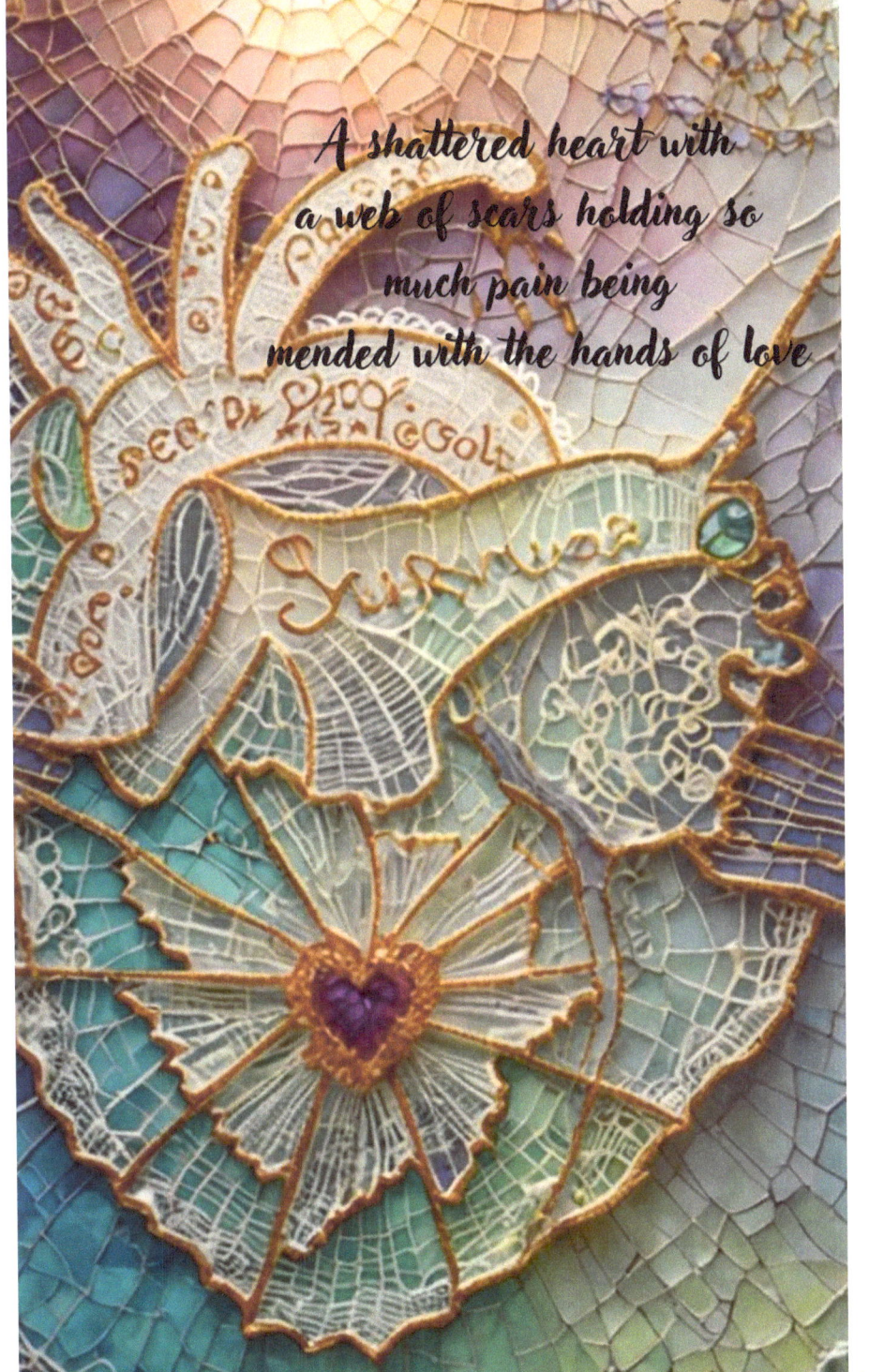

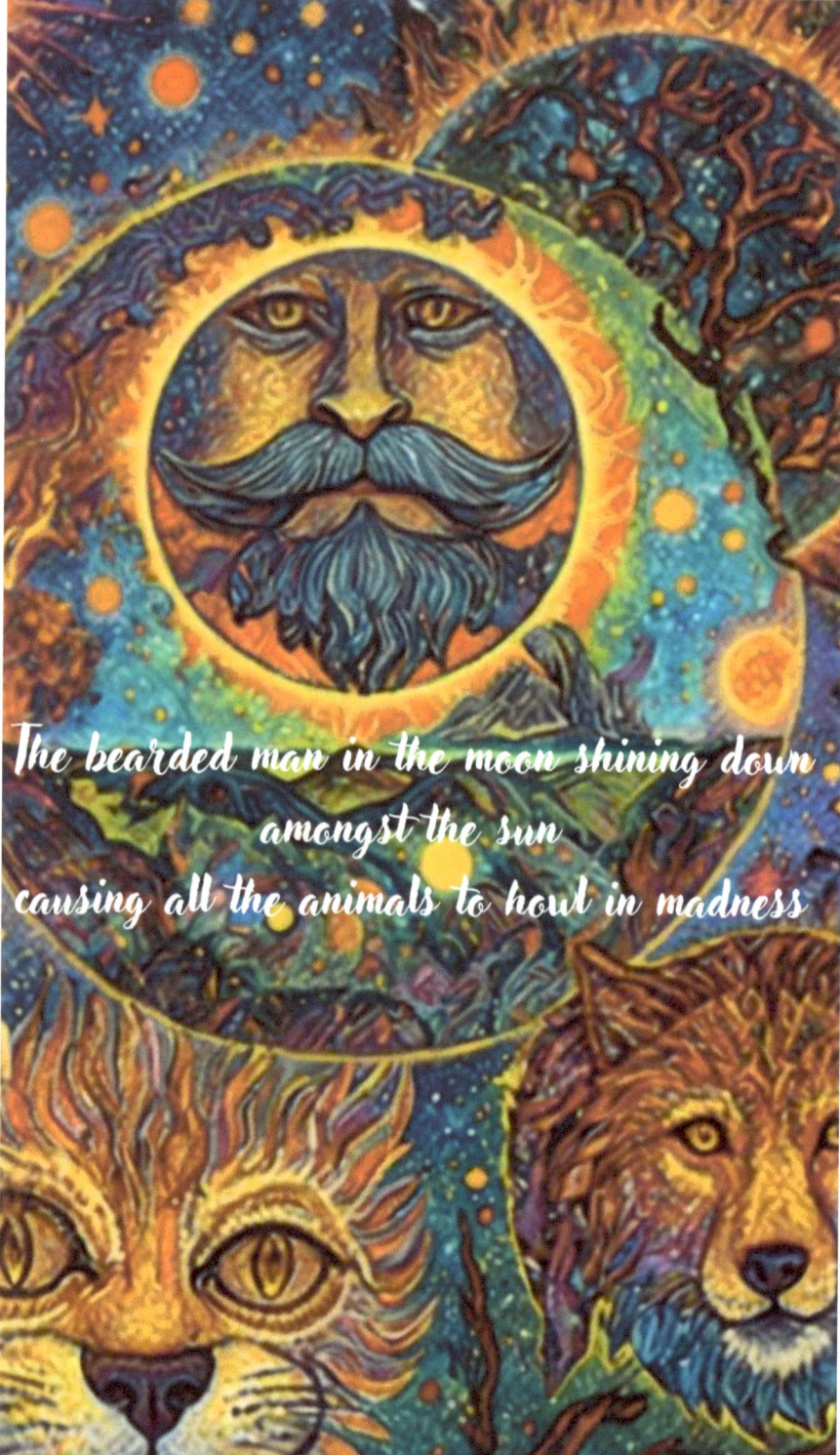

The bearded man in the moon shining down
amongst the sun
causing all the animals to howl in madness

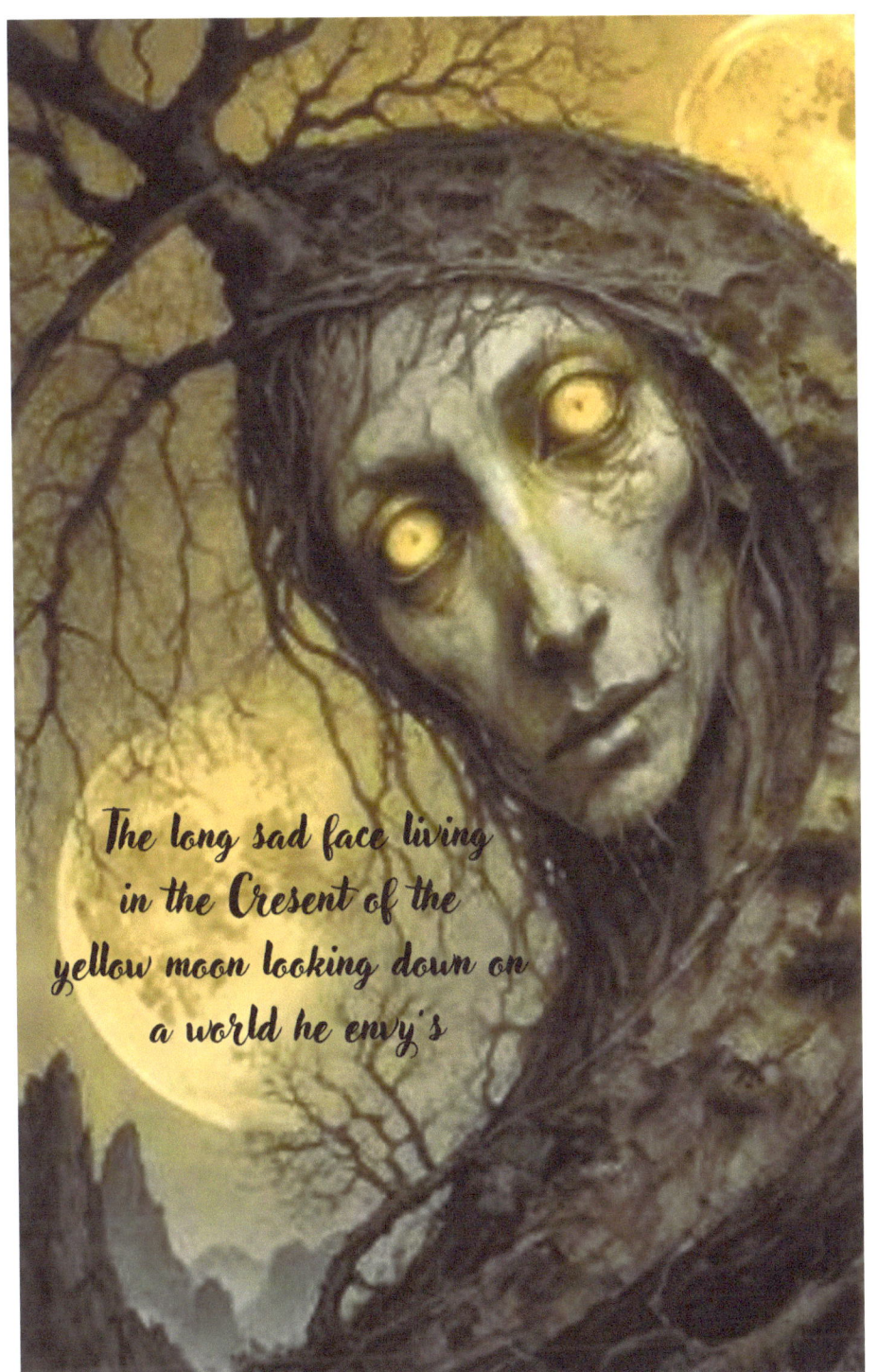

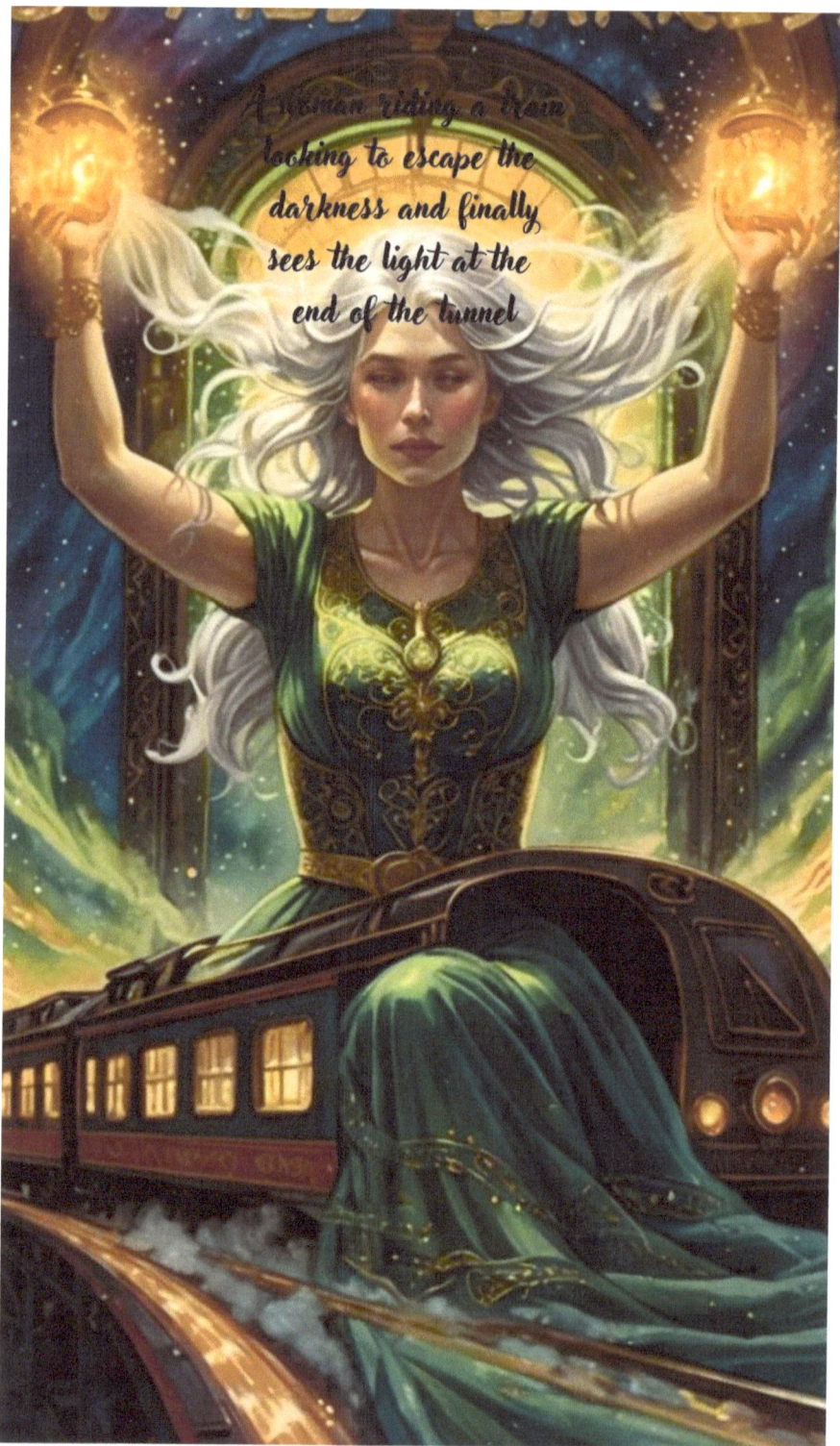

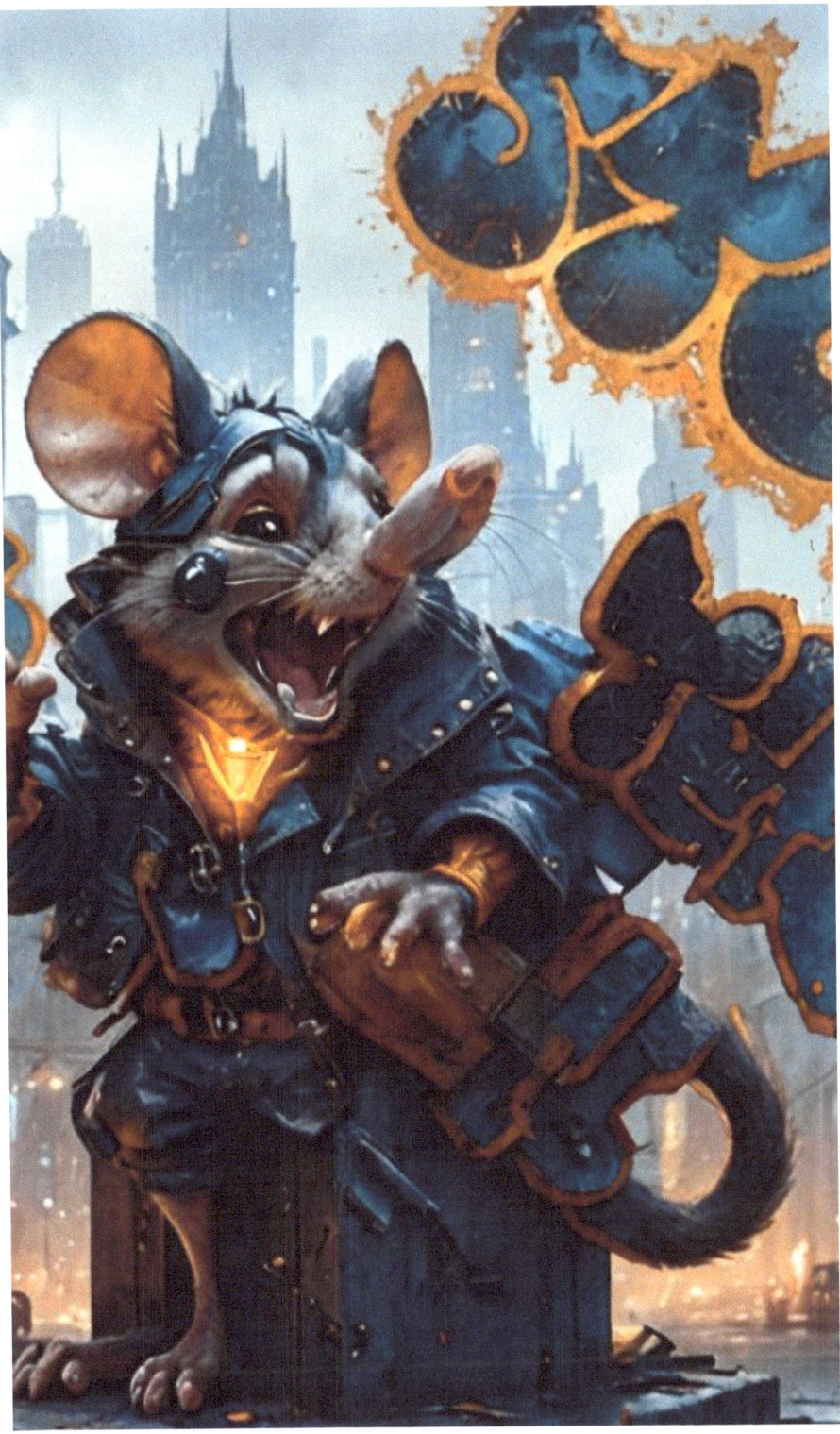

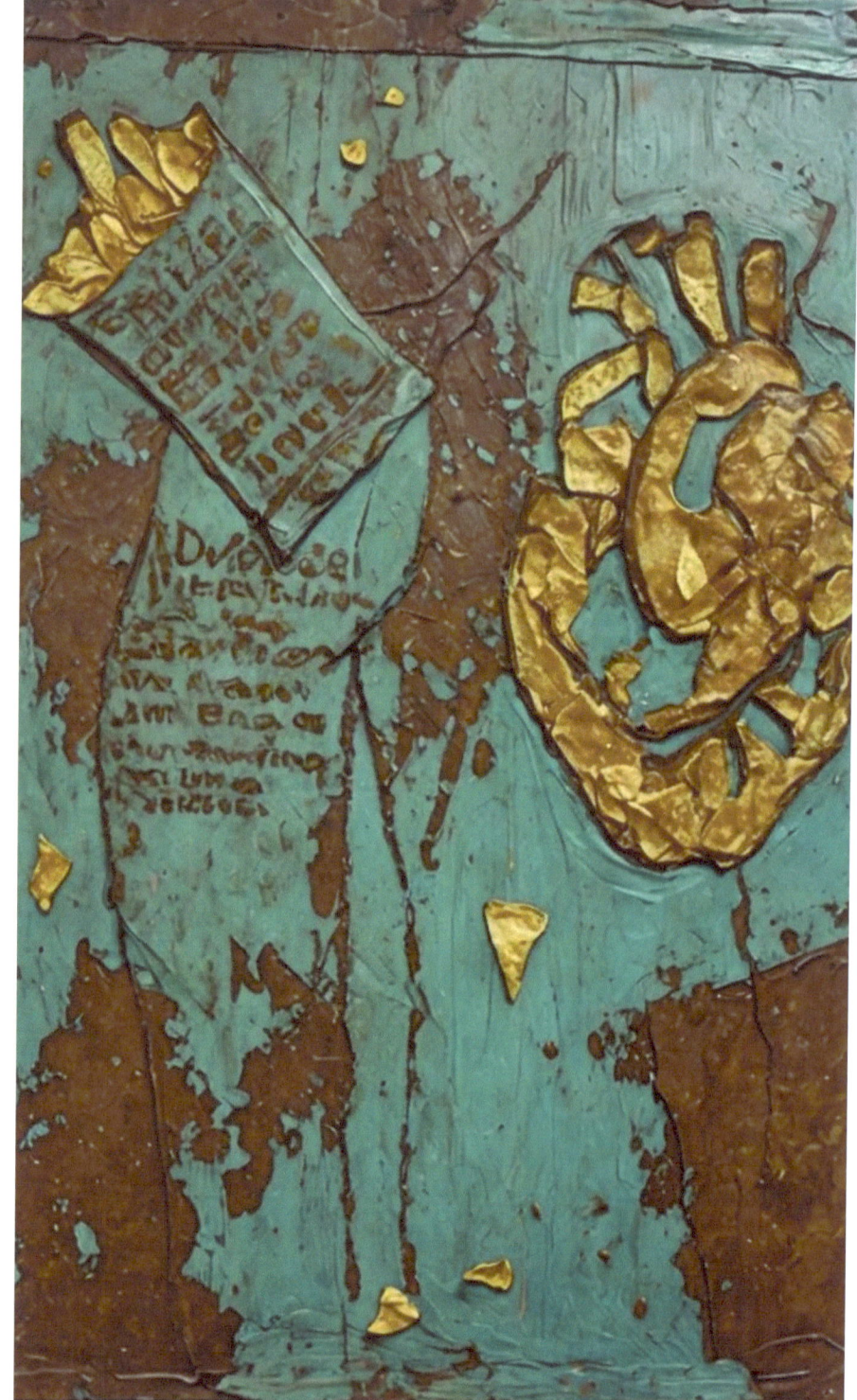

Wisdom Wall

23. God doesn't talk to you he talks through you
24. Know the truth and it will set you free
25. Wisdom is learning to be present in Gods presence
26. Old order has to vanish so all things become new
27. Old mindsets are dead
28. Become dead to sin and open to the truth of the Lord
29. Accusation to accusation needs to stop
30. Don't get bent out of shape from negative emotions
31. Nature of Christ makes all of us an agent of change
32. Wisdom is a win win what's received is given out
33. You lose the ability to worry when peace is available
34. Peace is the identity in the beloved
35. Give peace to the identity not the problem
36. We are born with all the fruits
37. Perfect peace is the absence of fear
38. Those who possess wisdom and give it away receive more
39. You don't need shame to change you only the goodness of Christ in you
40. When God creates he creates once and puts the ability for reproduction in oneself
41. The beginning of wisdom is the fear of God
42. Wisdom makes someone more beautiful
43. Welcoming correction makes for a brilliant mind
44. God judges the motives of the heart

Thanks For Your Purchase

Place your healing here

Place your healing here

www.ingramcontent.com/pod-product-compliance
Lightning Source LLC
Chambersburg PA
CBHW040055250526
45473CB00041B/618